All About
YOM KIPPUR

by
Judyth Groner
Madeline Wikler

illustrated by
Bonnie Gordon-Lucas

KAR-BEN COPIES, INC.
Rockville, MD

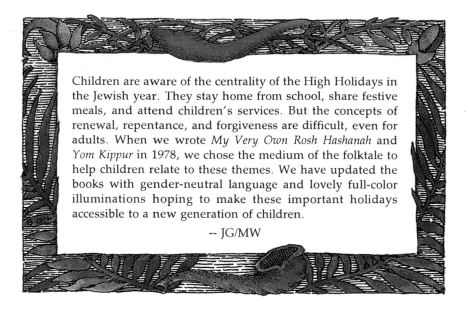

Children are aware of the centrality of the High Holidays in the Jewish year. They stay home from school, share festive meals, and attend children's services. But the concepts of renewal, repentance, and forgiveness are difficult, even for adults. When we wrote *My Very Own Rosh Hashanah* and *Yom Kippur* in 1978, we chose the medium of the folktale to help children relate to these themes. We have updated the books with gender-neutral language and lovely full-color illuminations hoping to make these important holidays accessible to a new generation of children.

-- JG/MW

Library of Congress Cataloging-in-Publication Data

Groner, Judyth Saypol
All About Yom Kippur / Judyth Groner and Madeline Wikler:
illustrated by Bonnie Gordon-Lucas.
p.   cm.
Summary: Brief text introduces the history and customs of Yom Kippur,
the Jewish Day of Forgiveness, the holiest day of the Jewish year.
Includes folktales.   ISBN 1-58013-005-4 (pbk.)
1. Yom Kippur — Juvenile literature. [1. Yom Kippur.]
I. Wikler, Madeline, 1943-
II. Gordon-Lucas, Bonnie, ill. III. Title.
BM695.A8G77   1997
296.4'32—dc21   97-2705
                                                                CIP
                                                                AC

Rosh Hashanah and Yom Kippur are a new beginning.

Why do we need a new beginning? Because —

> We do things we wish we had not done.
> We say things we wish we had not said.
> We make promises we may regret.
> We need a chance to start all over again.

Beginning on Rosh Hashanah, and for the next ten days, we think about the year that has passed and the year that is to come. On the tenth day we celebrate Yom Kippur, the Day of Forgiveness. It is the holiest day of the Jewish year.

Yom Kippur gives us a chance —

> To ask friends and family to forgive us.
> To forgive those who have made us angry.
> To make the new year better than last year.

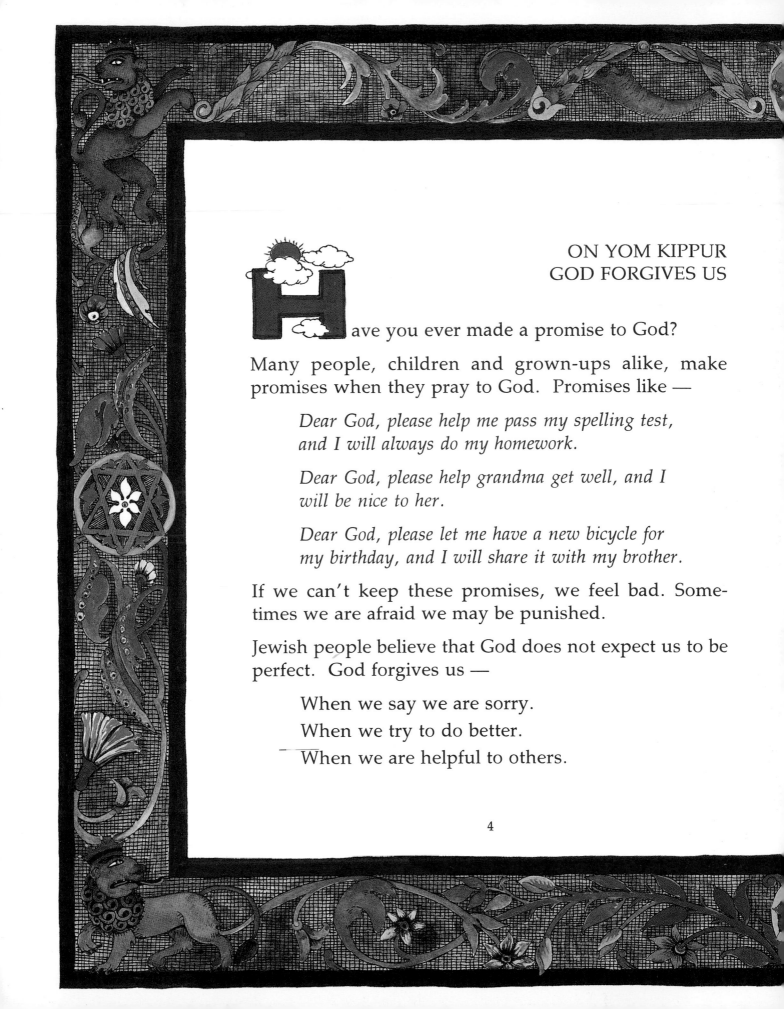

ON YOM KIPPUR
GOD FORGIVES US

Have you ever made a promise to God?

Many people, children and grown-ups alike, make promises when they pray to God. Promises like —

Dear God, please help me pass my spelling test, and I will always do my homework.

Dear God, please help grandma get well, and I will be nice to her.

Dear God, please let me have a new bicycle for my birthday, and I will share it with my brother.

If we can't keep these promises, we feel bad. Sometimes we are afraid we may be punished.

Jewish people believe that God does not expect us to be perfect. God forgives us —

When we say we are sorry.

When we try to do better.

When we are helpful to others.

4

ON YOM KIPPUR
WE FORGIVE EACH OTHER

But God can forgive us only for the promises we make to God. We also make promises to our friends and family.

> We promise our parents we will be helpful.
>
> We promise our friends we will play fairly.
>
> We promise our sisters and brothers we will share.
>
> We promise our teachers we will try harder.

Sometimes we can't keep these promises either. On Yom Kippur we have the chance to ask our friends and family to forgive us.

It is hard to ask forgiveness. It is hard to say, "I'm sorry." But it is important to say it and to mean it. It tells people we care about them.

It is even harder to forgive others when they hurt us. On Yom Kippur, just as we ask others to forgive us, we must try to forgive them. When someone says to us, "I'm sorry," we should say, "That's okay. Let's be friends again."

5

There was once a poor widow who had many children. They were always begging for food, but she had none to give them.

One day, while she was walking through the fields, she found an egg. She called her children together. "Look, children," she announced joyfully. "I have found an egg. We have nothing to worry about anymore.

"And being a wise woman, I will not let us eat the egg. I will ask our neighbor's permission to put it under her hen until it hatches into a baby chick.

"And we will not eat the baby chick, but will let it grow until it lays more eggs which will hatch into even more chicks.

"But we will not eat even these. Since I am such a wise woman, I will sell them and use the money to buy a cow. But we will not eat the cow. Instead, we will let it grow, and the cow will have baby calves.

"And since I am such a wise woman, I will sell them and use the money to buy a field. And we will have fields, and cows, and calves, and chickens, and eggs. And we will not be hungry anymore."

As the poor widow spoke, she turned the egg round and round in her hands. Suddenly it slipped, fell to the ground, and broke.

We are all like the country woman. We make many vows and promises. We say to ourselves, "I promise to do this," and "I promise to do that." But the days slip by, and often our promises do not lead to action.

YOM KIPPUR IS A FAST DAY

The Torah says that Yom Kippur is the holiest day of the Jewish year. It says that on this day —

We should not work.

We should pray and ask forgiveness.

We should punish ourselves.

This punishment has come to mean that we fast — we do not eat or drink.

Fasting on Yom Kippur gives us more time to think and pray, and helps us know how poor people feel when they are hungry.

Jewish law says that nothing is as important as life. Therefore, people who are too young, too old, or too sick are asked not to fast. But children may be taught how to fast, by skipping snacks or meals, until they build up the strength to fast for the whole day.

YOM KIPPUR AT HOME

 om Kippur begins in the evening with the Kol Nidre service. We eat an early dinner in order to arrive at the synagogue before sundown.

The meal before our fast is festive. Yom Kippur is a serious holiday, but it is not a sad one. We hope to be forgiven for our sins, and granted a new year filled with happiness and peace.

We eat our meal before the holiday begins, so we do not recite the *Kiddush*, the prayer over wine. We begin by dipping challah in honey as we did on Rosh Hashanah. After the meal, it is a custom to cover the table with Jewish books to show that we celebrate Yom Kippur not by eating, but by fasting and prayer.

In addition to lighting holiday candles, some families light *yarzheit*, memorial candles, to remember those who have died. These candles will burn through the night and all the next day.

KOL NIDRE

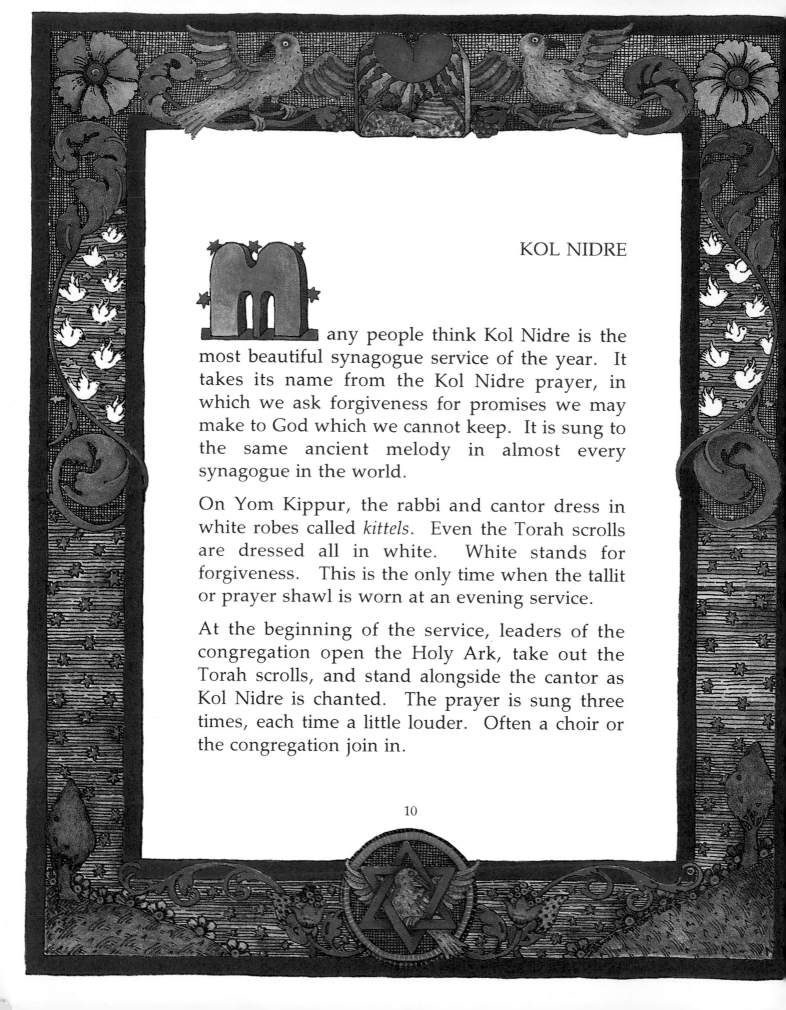

Many people think Kol Nidre is the most beautiful synagogue service of the year. It takes its name from the Kol Nidre prayer, in which we ask forgiveness for promises we may make to God which we cannot keep. It is sung to the same ancient melody in almost every synagogue in the world.

On Yom Kippur, the rabbi and cantor dress in white robes called *kittels*. Even the Torah scrolls are dressed all in white. White stands for forgiveness. This is the only time when the tallit or prayer shawl is worn at an evening service.

At the beginning of the service, leaders of the congregation open the Holy Ark, take out the Torah scrolls, and stand alongside the cantor as Kol Nidre is chanted. The prayer is sung three times, each time a little louder. Often a choir or the congregation join in.

ne Yom Kippur, a rabbi imagined he stood before God and had the following conversation:

God asked: "Have you studied all you should?"

The rabbi said, "No."

God asked: "Have you prayed all you should?"

Again the rabbi replied, "No."

God asked: "Have you done all the good deeds you should?"

This time, too, the rabbi replied, "No."

And God proclaimed: "You have told the truth, and for the sake of truth, you will be forgiven."

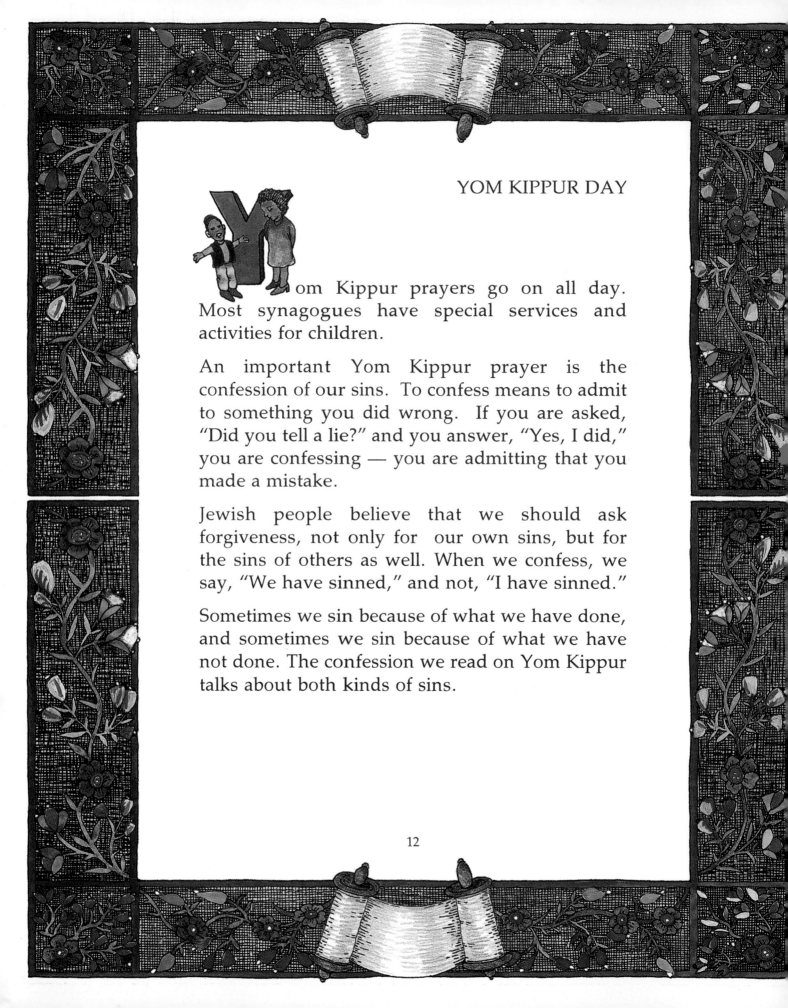

YOM KIPPUR DAY

Yom Kippur prayers go on all day. Most synagogues have special services and activities for children.

An important Yom Kippur prayer is the confession of our sins. To confess means to admit to something you did wrong. If you are asked, "Did you tell a lie?" and you answer, "Yes, I did," you are confessing — you are admitting that you made a mistake.

Jewish people believe that we should ask forgiveness, not only for our own sins, but for the sins of others as well. When we confess, we say, "We have sinned," and not, "I have sinned."

Sometimes we sin because of what we have done, and sometimes we sin because of what we have not done. The confession we read on Yom Kippur talks about both kinds of sins.

For the sins we have sinned before You, O God,

For gossiping and telling lies.
For being unfriendly or spiteful.
For wanting what someone else has.
For taking something that isn't ours.
For being rude to parents and teachers.
For causing another person to do wrong.

For not playing fairly.
For not keeping our promises.
For not admitting our mistakes.
For not accepting responsibility.
For not helping a person in trouble.
For not stopping someone from doing wrong.

For all of these sins, God of forgiveness,
Forgive us, pardon us, give us another chance.

nce there was a child who loved to gossip about her friends. Sometimes the stories she told were true, and sometimes the stories were not at all true. The neighborhood children were unhappy and decided to seek a rabbi's advice.

The rabbi heard their complaints and called the little girl to his house.

"Why do you make up stories about your friends?" the rabbi asked her.

"It's only talk," she replied. "I can always take it back."

"Perhaps you are right," said the rabbi, and he began to talk about other things.

When the child was ready to leave, the rabbi asked, "I wonder if you would do something for me."

"Of course," said the child.

The rabbi took a pillow from the couch and handed it to her. "Take this pillow to the town square," he said. "When you get there, cut it open, and shake out the feathers. Then come back here."

The child was puzzled, but agreed to do what the rabbi said. She carried the pillow to the town square and cut it open. The breeze scattered the feathers across the sky. When she returned to the rabbi's house and told him what she had done, the rabbi seemed pleased.

Then he handed the little girl a basket. "Now please go back to the square, and gather the feathers up again," he told her.

The child gasped. "But that's impossible," she said.

"You are right," said the rabbi. "It is also not possible to take back all the untrue things you say about others. You must be careful with the words you speak. Once sent on their way, they cannot be gathered again."

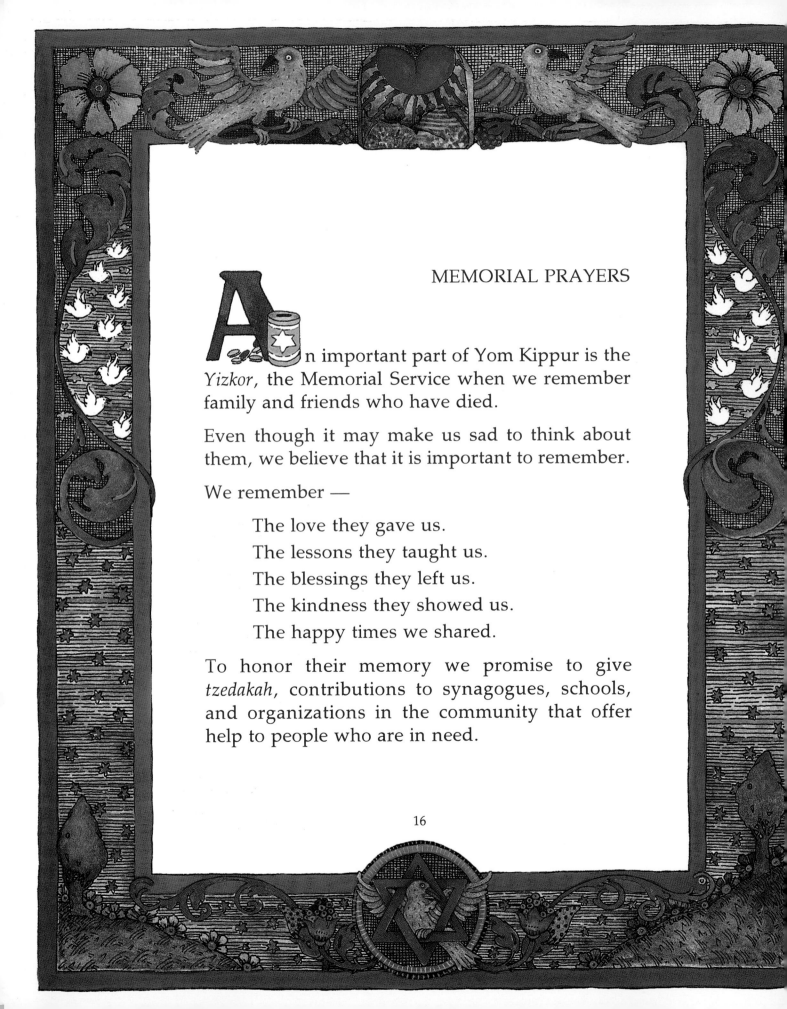

MEMORIAL PRAYERS

An important part of Yom Kippur is the *Yizkor*, the Memorial Service when we remember family and friends who have died.

Even though it may make us sad to think about them, we believe that it is important to remember.

We remember —

> The love they gave us.
> The lessons they taught us.
> The blessings they left us.
> The kindness they showed us.
> The happy times we shared.

To honor their memory we promise to give *tzedakah*, contributions to synagogues, schools, and organizations in the community that offer help to people who are in need.

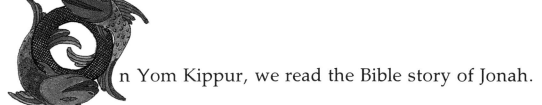

O n Yom Kippur, we read the Bible story of Jonah.

God spoke to Jonah and told him to go to the city of Nineveh to warn the wicked people there to change their ways. But Jonah did not want to go. Instead he boarded a ship bound for another city. When a big rainstorm rocked the ship, Jonah knew that God had found him. He knew the storm was his fault and told the sailors to throw him into the sea. They did, and the storm stopped.

God sent a huge fish to swallow Jonah. Jonah lived in the belly of the fish for three days and nights. With time to think and pray, he realized that he could not hide from God.

God caused the fish to let Jonah go free. This time when God told Jonah to go to Nineveh, he went. He warned the people to stop their evil ways. They began to behave better, and God did not punish them.

The story of Jonah teaches us that God wants us to change our ways. God wants to forgive us.

ong ago in a small village there lived a young boy. He had difficulty learning and could not read or write. As a shepherd, he spent his days watching his sheep and playing his flute, which he loved very much.

One year he begged his father to let him go to synagogue on Yom Kippur. He tucked his flute in his coat pocket.

The boy sat in the synagogue all day and listened to the beautiful praying and singing. He wanted to join in, but did not know how to pray. Then he remembered his flute and asked his father if he could play it for God. His father warned the boy not to disturb the congregation.

During the afternoon service the boy asked again if he could play his flute, and again his father warned him not to.

Finally the time came for the cantor to chant the Neilah service, the closing prayers for Yom Kippur.

Suddenly the boy could not hold back any longer. He took the flute from his pocket, put it to his lips, and played the sound that he felt in his heart.

His father became angry. But the rabbi turned to him and said, "All Yom Kippur, I have prayed hard so that our sins might be forgiven. But I felt that my prayers were not heard. When your little boy played on his flute, I knew at once the gates of heaven had opened.

"The boy's simple song to God came from his heart, and through him, all our prayers were lifted to heaven."

All during Yom Kippur we pray that the gates of heaven will be open to let in our prayers. The final service of the day is called *Neilah*, which means closing—the closing of Yom Kippur and the closing of the gates of heaven.

We end the service by reciting the *Shema* affirming our belief in God as judge.

שְׁמַע יִשְׂרָאֵל יְיָ אֱלֹהֵינוּ יְיָ אֶחָד.

Shema Yisrael Adonai Eloheinu Adonai Echad.

Hear O Israel, Adonai is our God, Adonai alone.

After one long blast of the shofar — *Tekiyah Gedolah!* — we wish each other a good new year and hurry home to end our fast. Following the meal, it is a custom to begin preparations for *Sukkot*, the harvest holiday which begins the next week.

Home Service for
YOM KIPPUR

TZEDAKAH

Giving *tzedakah*, sharing what we have, is one way of asking forgiveness on Yom Kippur.

On the afternoon before the holiday, many synagogues set out plates on a large table. Each plate has the name of a Jewish school, hospital, or other organization. Those who come to recite afternoon prayers put money into each of the plates.

We also give *tzedakah* to honor the memory of friends and family who have died.

Before we share the meal before the fast, we can set aside some of our savings for *tzedakah*.

HAMOTZI
CHALLAH BLESSING

The meal before Yom Kippur is especially festive, because soon we will begin our fast. As we share the challah, we are grateful for the blessings of life, health, and friendship.

בָּרוּךְ אַתָּה יְיָ אֱלֹהֵינוּ מֶלֶךְ הָעוֹלָם,
הַמוֹצִיא לֶחֶם מִן הָאָרֶץ.

Baruch Atah Adonai Eloheinu Melech ha'olam,
Hamotzi lechem min ha'aretz.

Thank You, God,
for the blessing of bread,
and for the festive meal
which we will now enjoy together.

BIRKAT HAMAZON
AFTER THE MEAL

We join in giving thanks for the meal we have eaten.

בָּרוּךְ אַתָּה יְיָ, הַזָּן אֶת־הַכֹּל.

Baruch Atah Adonai hazan et hakol.

עֹשֶׂה שָׁלוֹם בִּמְרוֹמָיו הוּא יַעֲשֶׂה שָׁלוֹם
עָלֵינוּ וְעַל כָּל־יִשְׂרָאֵל. וְאִמְרוּ אָמֵן.

*Oseh shalom bimromav hu ya'aseh shalom
Aleinu v'al kol Yisrael ve'imru amen.*

Thank you, God,
for the festive meal we have shared,
for the food we have eaten at this table,
for the Torah and mitzvot which guide our lives,
for Israel, the homeland of the Jewish people,
for our freedom to live as Jews,
for life, strength, and health.
Hear our prayers, and grant us forgiveness.

BIRKAT HABANIM
CHILDREN'S BLESSING

On Yom Kippur eve, before going to synagogue, parents set aside time to bless their children and bestow the traditional priestly blessing.

יְבָרֶכְךָ יְיָ וְיִשְׁמְרֶךָ.
יָאֵר יְיָ פָּנָיו אֵלֶיךָ וִיחֻנֶּךָּ.
יִשָּׂא יְיָ פָּנָיו אֵלֶיךָ וְיָשֵׂם לְךָ שָׁלוֹם.

Y'varechecha Adonai v'yishmerecha.
Ya'er Adonai panav elecha vichuneka.
Yisa Adonai panav elecha v'yasem l'cha shalom.

May God bless and keep you.
May God watch over you in kindness.
May God grant you a life
of good health, joy, and peace.

HADLAKAT NEROT
CANDLE-LIGHTING

Before leaving for synagogue, we welcome the festival of Yom Kippur with the lighting of the candles.

בָּרוּךְ אַתָּה יְיָ אֱלֹהֵינוּ מֶלֶךְ הָעוֹלָם,
אֲשֶׁר קִדְּשָׁנוּ בְּמִצְוֹתָיו וְצִוָּנוּ
לְהַדְלִיק נֵר שֶׁל (שַׁבָּת וְשֶׁל) יוֹם הַכִּפֻּרִים.

Baruch Atah Adonai Eloheinu Melech ha'olam,
Asher kid'shanu b'mitzvotav v'tzivanu
L'hadlik ner shel (Shabbat v'shel) Yom Hakippurim.

בָּרוּךְ אַתָּה יְיָ אֱלֹהֵינוּ מֶלֶךְ הָעוֹלָם,
שֶׁהֶחֱיָנוּ וְקִיְּמָנוּ וְהִגִּיעָנוּ לַזְּמַן הַזֶּה.

Baruch Atah Adonai Eloheinu Melech ha'olam,
Shehecheyanu, vekiy'manu v'higiyanu laz'man hazeh.

Thank you, God,
for bringing our family together
to celebrate Yom Kippur,
and for the mitzvah of lighting the candles.

May You forgive us and help us to forgive others.
May You bless us with a year of peace.

BIRKAT HAMAZON

M. NATHANSON

OSEH SHALOM

By N. HIRSH

LIGHTING THE CANDLES

Freely adapted after a version by A.W. BINDER

Freely, as a chant

Ba - ruch a - tah a - do nai e - lo - hei - nu me - lech ha -

o - lam, a - sher kid - sha - nu b'mitz - vo - tav v'tzi - va - nu l' - had - lik

ner, l' had - lik ner, shel Yom Ha - kip - pur - im.

SHEHECHEYANU

Traditional

Ba - ruch a - tah a - do - nai e - lo - hei - nu me - lech ha - o - lam she -

he - che - ya - nu v' - kiy' - ma - nu v' - hi - gi - ya - nu la - z'man ha - zeh.

L'SHANAH TOVAH

Traditional

L' - sha - nah to - vah ti - ka - te - vu, l' - sha - nah to - vah ti - ka -

te - vu, ti - ka - te - vu v' - te - cha - te - mu.

KOL NIDRE

Traditional

Kol nid - re —— v' - e - sa - re —— v' - cha - ra - me —— v' - ko - na -

me —— v' - chi - nu - ye —— v' - ki - nu - se —— u - sh' - vu - ot.

LET'S BE FRIENDS

G. GEWIRTZ

Let's be friends, make a - mends, now's the time to say I'm sor - ry.

Let's be friends, make a - mends, please say you'll for - give me. The — give me.

ten days of te - shu - vah, time to make up time to pray. —

Shake my hand, I'll — shake yours. Let's be friends for al - ways.

AVINU MALKENU

Traditional

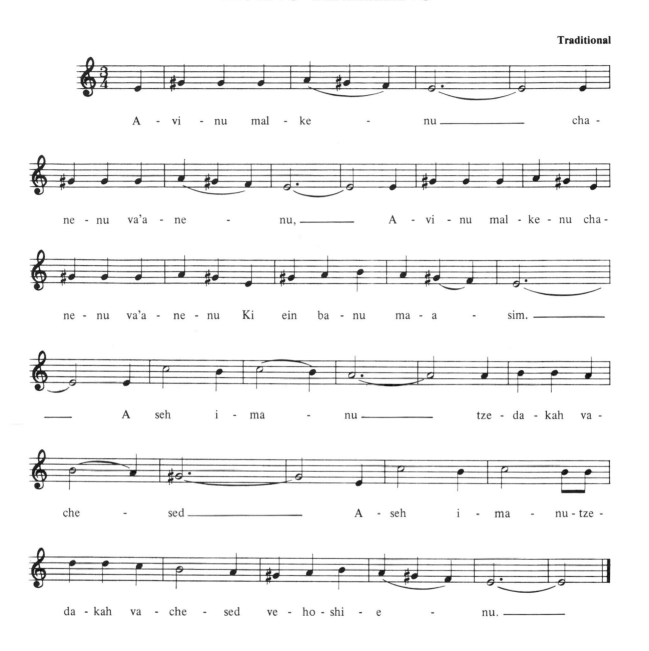

A - vi - nu mal - ke - nu _____ cha -

ne - nu va'a - ne - nu, _____ A - vi - nu mal - ke - nu cha -

ne - nu va'a - ne - nu Ki ein ba - nu ma - a - sim. _____

_____ A seh i - ma - nu _____ tze - da - kah va -

che - sed _____ A - seh i - ma - nu - tze -

da - kah va - che - sed ve - ho - shi - e - nu. _____

Also from Kar-Ben...

HIGH HOLIDAY FAMILY SERVICES

  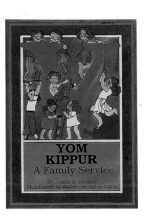

Creative, attractive, and affordable prayerbooks for the high holidays written by Rabbi Judith Z. Abrams; art by Katherine Janus Kahn; words and music to original songs by Cantor Frances T. Goldman.

Built around the concepts of *tefillah* (prayer), *teshuvah* (repentance), and *tzedakah* (sharing), the services include stories and pictures to capture the attention of young children and prayers and readings to challenge older children and adults. *Songs for the High Holidays*, a companion cassette, features words and music to original songs plus traditional holiday melodies.

At your bookstore or call
1-800-4-KARBEN (1-800-452-7236)